DISCARD

BIOG JOHNSON

Judy Johnson

Kathleen Billus

Published in 2002 by The Rosen Publishing Group, Inc.
29 East 21st Street, New York, NY 10010

Copyright © 2002 by The Rosen Publishing Group, Inc.

First Edition

All rights reserved. No part of this book may be reproduced in any form without permission in writing from the publisher, except by a reviewer.

Library of Congress Cataloging-in-Publication Data

Billus, Kathleen.
  Judy Johnson / Kathleen Billus.— 1st ed.
    p. cm. — (Baseball Hall of Famers of the Negro Leagues)
  Includes bibliographical references (p.) and index.
  Summary: Presents the life of the famed Negro League third baseman and discusses segregation in America, the formation of the Negro Leagues, and the integration of professional baseball in 1947.
  ISBN 0-8239-3476-4 (lib. bdg.)
  1. Johnson, Judy, 1900–1989—Juvenile literature. 2. Baseball players—United States—Biography—Juvenile literature. 3. African American baseball players—Biography—Juvenile literature. 4. Negro leagues—Juvenile literature. [1. Johnson, Judy, 1900–1989. 2. Baseball players. 3. African Americans—Biography. 4. Negro leagues.]
  I. Title. II. Series.
  GV865.J598 B55 2002
  796.357'092—dc21
                                                           2001003571

Manufactured in the United States of America

Contents

Introduction	5
1. Born to Play Baseball	10
2. The Negro Leagues	20
3. The Rookie	43
4. Highs and Lows	62
5. Life After the Crawfords	74
6. Remembering Judy Johnson	86
Timeline	100
Glossary	102
For More Information	105
For Further Reading	107
Index	109

Although Judy Johnson never made it to the major leagues, he is considered to be one of the best baseball players ever.

Introduction

Judy Johnson would one day be recognized as one of the greatest players in the history of baseball. But such recognition took longer than it should have. Johnson was born with exceptional gifts and athletic ability, but he was also born an African American man, a "Negro" in a white America. Although his carefree boyhood memories and early athletic talent seemed to indicate that his future would be filled with opportunities to play the game he loved more than almost anything, he faced a huge obstacle blocking his path. This obstacle stood in the way of all African American baseball players and all African American people in the United States. No matter how good or caring or talented

Judy Johnson

or skilled, all African American men, women, and children faced racial discrimination and segregation in their own country. Because of a law forbidding African Americans and whites from living and working together, African Americans in many areas of the country were not allowed to use "white" restaurants, hotels, train cars, and water fountains. And because he wasn't white, Judy Johnson could not play baseball professionally in the major leagues.

Even though slavery was abolished in the 1860s after the Civil War, African Americans were treated little better as free men and women than they had been treated as slaves. Racial discrimination against African Americans and other people of color was the common practice throughout most of the country, especially in the South. In 1896, the U.S. Supreme Court's verdict in the *Plessy v. Ferguson* trial ruled that an African American man could be arrested for refusing to leave a "whites only" railroad car. The Supreme Court ruled that segregation of races was a constitutional right as long as the facilities for

Introduction

An African American man drinks from a water fountain labeled "colored."

both races were equal. "Separate but equal" became the excuse racist whites could use in order to avoid having to live, work, or do business with African Americans. Under *Plessy v. Ferguson,* African Americans could be legally barred from white restaurants, schools, drinking fountains, and other public places because, as the law stated, they could have their own restaurants, schools, and drinking fountains. However, in most cases,

Judy Johnson

those facilities were in no way equal. Whites-only restaurants and drinking fountains were of far better quality than were the restaurants and drinking fountains African Americans could use.

The separate-but-equal laws were also known as Jim Crow laws. The name "Jim Crow" refers to a popular nineteenth-century song about an African American named Jim Crow who happily accepts poor treatment from white people. Sadly,

Under segregation, a black woman could be arrested for sitting on one of these park benches in Paris, Tennessee, which were designated for "white women only."

Introduction

Jim Crow laws legally repressed African Americans and all other people of color in the United States until 1965, when the Civil Rights Act was passed prohibiting discrimination on the basis of race.

The story of Judy Johnson's life is a remarkable look back at a sports hero who lived life to the fullest, played the game he loved, and always remembered to treat people as equals. He believed that everyone deserved his kindness, generosity, and intelligence, even if many people in his own country treated him and his fellow African Americans as second-class citizens. Judy Johnson was one of best pinch-hitting third basemen who ever played baseball. Those who saw him play were amazed with his talent on the diamond. He won admiration, respect, and also affection. Johnson was known by the nickname Judy, but many people he met also called him Mr. Sunshine for the warmth and hope he carried with him like rays of sunshine.

Born to Play Baseball

William Julius "Judy" Johnson was born the second of three children on October 26, 1899, in Snow Hill, Maryland, to William Henry Johnson and Annie Lee Johnson. He was called Billy up to the age of nineteen, when he was given the nickname Judy. When Johnson was about ten years old, his father, who was a sailor by trade, moved the Johnson family from Maryland to Wilmington, Delaware. There William Johnson, a sports enthusiast, became the athletic director of Wilmington's Negro Settlement House. William Johnson encouraged all three of his children to play sports. Looking back at his childhood,

Born to Play Baseball

Judy Johnson said that his father always filled the backyard with lots of sports and play equipment, such as jungle gyms and monkey bars. Johnson said his backyard had "everything you'd find in a gym." The Johnsons' backyard wasn't anything like the typical backyard of the average American family living in the early part of the 1900s. Today, backyard swing sets and slides and jungle gyms are in almost every suburban child's backyard, but this equipment was an extremely rare sight during Johnson's childhood. Judy Johnson was probably the only kid on the block to have a playground in his backyard!

William Johnson strongly encouraged young Judy to participate in sports. But he wasn't thinking about baseball as the perfect sport for his son to play. Boxing was William's favorite sport, and he spent a lot of time in the ring as a boxing trainer at the Negro Settlement House. William hoped that Judy would become a prizefighter someday. When Judy was only eight years old, his dad went

Judy Johnson

out and bought two pairs of boxing gloves. Then he set up boxing matches between Judy and his older sister, Mary Emma. Poor little Judy Johnson was no match for Mary Emma, who was a strong, athletic twelve-year-old. Mary Emma was much older, taller, and bigger than her little brother. Imagine what it would be like to be in Judy's shoes—an eight-year-old boy forced by your own father into a boxing match with your twelve-year-old sister. Maybe some boys might have enjoyed such a boxing match. Maybe some boys might have seized it as an opportunity to beat up their sisters with their dads' permission; not Judy Johnson. He wanted nothing to do with this boxing match. When Mary Emma came at him swinging, throwing punches hard and fast, Judy didn't know what to do. He figured he couldn't hit her in the face, chest, or stomach. Whether those places were illegal punch zones or not, Judy said that he just felt plain bad about hitting a girl, even if his dad was telling him to punch and jab at her. Judy ended up taking far more punches than he landed on Mary Emma. No matter how hard his sister hit him, he couldn't shake the notion that a boy shouldn't ever hit a girl, even if she was punching the stuffing out of him. Judy didn't have the heart to fight his sister. His heart wasn't in boxing, period. Judy Johnson's heart was in baseball.

Playing in the Park

Fortunately for both Judy Johnson and the history of baseball, his father didn't force him to pursue a boxing career. Johnson started playing baseball when he was in elementary school, when he and his friends would play baseball every day after school in the field behind his backyard. Since his father was the athletic director for Wilmington's Negro Settlement House, Johnson always had plenty of sports equipment, much more than most of his friends. Bats and balls were plentiful. He sometimes wondered if the neighborhood kids included him in their games not because of his talent as a ballplayer (he claimed he wasn't good when he started out), but because his father always provided the sports equipment. Johnson was always modest and low-key about his talents, more willing to give others credit than himself. Maybe he didn't start out playing baseball like a pro, but after years of play and practice, he certainly improved.

Johnson and the neighborhood boys spent most of their free time playing ball at Delmar Place, not far from his house. Delmar Place was a field right behind the park that would later be dedicated to Johnson in 1975, the year he was inducted into the major league Baseball Hall of Fame. The field was a pasture where cows and sheep grazed all day, until Johnson and his friends arrived after school and shooed the animals off the field so they could play game after game until sunset.

Born to Play Baseball

Johnson's dad coached a local baseball team called the Royal Blues. Young Judy served the team as batboy until he was old enough to join. When Johnson first joined the Royal Blues, he played with his father's old baseball glove. This was Johnson's first real glove, but it didn't fit well at all; it slipped off constantly. Worse yet, the leather glove had become badly damaged from dry rot, but Johnson kept it anyway and used it until it nearly fell apart. His father soon replaced the tattered glove with a new one.

Johnson's first baseball shoes were even worse. He bought some metal spikes and took them to a shoemaker to have them placed on a pair of his street shoes. Evidently, Johnson neglected to remove the heels from the shoes before dropping them off at the shoemaker, and the shoemaker nailed all the spikes all over the bottom of the shoes, even through the heel. With the spikes in, the heels added too much height to the shoes, forcing Johnson to

Innovations Credited to African American Baseball

Chest padding: African American Negro league umpire John Craig created a chest protector by stuffing sponges between squares of cardboard, which was worn inside his coat.

Shin guards: Second baseman Bud Fowler grew tired of being cut by players' shoe spikes. He created guards to protect his shins by taping pieces of wood to his legs.

Lighting for night games: Kansas City Monarchs team owner J. L. Wilkinson is known as the Father of Night Baseball. In 1930, Wilkinson designed a lighting system so big it was carried into the park by truck. Lights were attached to fifty-foot telescoping poles. The system was connected to a huge generator. Attendance ballooned to crowds of 10,000 to 12,000 fans.

lean forward at a sharp angle. He couldn't walk! He couldn't even stand up straight! Compared to his first baseball gloves and shoes, Johnson's first uniform was no problem: His mother sewed it herself.

Negro league umpires John Craig *(left)* **and M. Moe Harris stand on the field before a game.**

The Rosedale Years

Although Johnson loved playing baseball, he also appreciated the fringe benefit of being on his school's baseball team—he and his teammates were excused from classes five minutes early on game days. When Johnson reached early adolescence, he joined an organized amateur baseball team called the Rosedales. The Rosedales played local teams every Saturday. They even competed against some white clubs in addition to three or four other African American teams. They often played two or three games in one day and would walk as a team from one field to the next.

After every game, Johnson went to the team captain's house to hang out. He quickly developed a big crush on the captain's sister, Anita, who would later become his wife. It seemed obvious to everyone that he wasn't visiting the captain so often because he wanted merely to talk baseball or hang out with teammates; he was there to spend time with Anita. Johnson would stay with Anita as long as he could until her father coughed loudly, which was the signal for Johnson to go home. In response to the signal, Anita walked Johnson to the street corner, where he would give her a quick kiss good-bye. For Johnson, finding his soul mate was like finding baseball: It was love at first sight. Johnson said, "Next to my wife, I loved baseball best."

The Negro Leagues

In the 1880s, both African Americans and whites eagerly played baseball. In 1867, a group of team organizers had formed the National Association of Base Ball Players (which became the National League), which banned African American players from their teams. For at least twenty years, however, African Americans still managed to play on teams with whites. In 1884, Moses Fleetwood Walker became the first African American player to join a major league team, Ohio's Toledo Blue Stockings. Walker faced racism from players on his own team as well as those on the opposing teams. In 1887, Cap Anson, the white manager of the major league Chicago

Cap Anson was the first manager to draw a color line, excluding African Americans from playing major league baseball.

Judy Johnson

White Stockings, said that neither he nor his players would ever play on a team with African Americans. Ball clubs soon stopped signing African American players entirely. Until the color barrier was broken in 1947, African Americans and whites would play only on opposing teams, and only in exhibition games.

By 1900, professional baseball became completely segregated. White major league owners claimed that they had no choice but to ban African American players because, they said, southern white teams would never play teams that included African American players. Other racist defenses included claims that there simply weren't enough good African American players to go around. Many owners stuck to racially segregated teams simply because the profit potential was far better: Some owners figured that they could make extra money by renting out their stadiums and parks to African American teams when their own teams were on the road. In any case, *Plessy v. Ferguson* had made this sort of division perfectly legal. African Americans had effectively been shut out of playing professional baseball in their own country.

Rube Foster

In 1911, former pitcher Andrew "Rube" Foster joined forces with a white bar owner named John Schorling. Together they founded the all–African American team, the Chicago American Giants. Foster was part-owner of the Chicago American Giants as well as its manager.

During a nationwide epidemic of race riots in 1919, Rube Foster laid the groundwork for the Negro National League. He wanted to make sure that African American baseball and its players retained some control over themselves and their earnings. He also believed that creating a national league would establish credibility for African American baseball players. There was a white major league, so why not a Negro league? A smart businessman, Foster figured the league would make money by developing intercity rivalries

Judy Johnson

and promoting a world series. He hoped that working with team owners across the country would prevent them from stealing players from other teams. Foster thought that an association of baseball teams would result in the construction of new ballparks, player development, a stable game schedule, and better competition. He wanted the Negro league to improve the social status of African American ballplayers and increase opportunities for African Americans in other baseball-related jobs, such as scouts and umpires.

Foster was indeed a visionary, and his idea would eventually take off. But there were problems at first. For one thing, there wasn't enough financial support. Some teams, such as Ohio's Dayton Marcos, were forced to disband because of lack of money. There also weren't enough smart managers to go around. Few teams owned their own ballpark, and two teams had no home field to play on and only played road games. Scheduling was difficult to straighten out. Most teams rented parks from

The Negro Leagues

minor league teams and could only use them when those teams were traveling to other cities.

By 1921, Rube Foster was frustrated with weak team managers who let themselves be bullied by team owners, often selling and buying players left and right. In 1923, a number of African American teams from the East formed the Eastern Colored League (ECL). The Brooklyn Royal Giants (New York), the Philadelphia Hilldales (Pennsylvania), the Lincoln Giants (New York), the Atlantic City Bacharach Giants (New Jersey), the Baltimore African American Sox (Maryland), and the Cuban All Stars (New York) made up the ECL. The first Negro League World Series in 1924 featured the Philadelphia Hilldales (with Judy Johnson) against the Kansas City Monarchs. The Monarchs won after a ten-game contest.

The Eastern Colored League stole away players from the Negro National League constantly, and Rube Foster's finances were doing as poorly as his health. Foster suffered a

Judy Johnson

nervous breakdown in 1926 and never recovered. He died in 1930 at the age of fifty-one. After his death, Judge W. C. Hueston became the new president of the Negro National League, but could not fill Foster's shoes. The League folded in 1932 (as did the Eastern Colored League), but was rescued and reorganized by Gus Greenlee. The new Negro National League formed in 1933, and it included the Pittsburgh Crawfords (Pennsylvania), the Homestead Grays (Pennsylvania), the Indianapolis ABCs (Indiana), the Detroit Stars (Michigan), the Columbus Blue Birds (Ohio), and the Chicago American Giants (Illinois). In 1938, Greenlee's Negro National League joined up with the new Negro American League, whose teams included the Jacksonville Red Caps (Florida), the Atlanta Black Crackers (Georgia), the Memphis Red Sox (Tennessee), and the Birmingham Black Barons (Alabama). Other African American leagues existed as well, including the Texas Negro League and the

Gus Greenlee was one of the driving forces behind the success of the Negro leagues.

Pitching Tricks: "Doctoring the Ball"

The Spitter: A pitch made with a ball that has been spat upon, causing it to dip sharply.

The Shineball: A pitched ball that has been made very smooth by rubbing it with Vaseline or some other smoothing agent, causing it to dip sharply as it nears home plate.

The Emery Ball: A pitched ball that has been roughed up with emery cloth or sandpaper, causing the ball to move erratically as it nears home plate.

Negro Southern League, which were mostly semiprofessional African American leagues.

Winter Leagues

Since the Negro leagues didn't pay its players enough money to live on for the entire year, many players spent their winters playing baseball in Latin America. Cuba, Mexico, Puerto Rico, and Venezuela were especially popular locations for winter play. The lifestyles of the ballplayers were easier in Latin America because players didn't have to travel to different cities as often as they did in the

The Negro Leagues

United States. Also, teams only played three games a week at the most. The schedule was ideal in many ways: Players could continue practicing their baseball skills and still have time for some rest and relaxation before spring training back in the states.

Homestead Grays pitcher Ray Brown *(left)* chats with a Cuban baseball player during a winter game.

In Latin America, African Americans and whites played together. These countries were integrated both on and off the field. There were no Jim Crow laws to deal with; African American ballplayers were treated just as well as white ballplayers. In addition, many African American players were even considered heroes and were treated with respect by both the Latin American ballplayers and the audiences. They were able to stay in the best hotels, and not in segregated quarters. In Latin America, they received star treatment and were also paid a lot more than they were in the United States. As a result, many African American players ended up making half of their entire salaries in just a few months playing outside of the United States. Some players even moved to Latin America permanently to play ball.

Barnstorming

At the end of the regular baseball season, white major leaguers traveled around the country playing exhibition games. This was known as barnstorming. African American baseball teams went on barnstorming tours all year long. While white teams barnstormed to make some extra money, African American teams barnstormed year-round to earn most of their annual income. For the African American teams, barnstorming

> **"Deducts"**
>
> African American baseball players often saw all kinds of mysterious expenses deducted from their paychecks. They were told that all players were required to pay these fees, or "deducts," for various ballpark services such as umpire salaries, park fees, and even police service.

wasn't an optional activity; it was the key to their survival.

Barnstorming teams typically played three kinds of games: games against teams in their league; games against local semiprofessional teams; and games purely for entertainment purposes. When African American teams played these exhibition games, no one paid attention to the score. They only paid attention to the teams' skills and style. For example, the Zulu Giants wore uniforms with grass skirts. The Indianapolis Clowns wore clown makeup.

But even when Negro league teams went back to playing real games that were scored,

Judy Johnson

the men played with more fun and humor than did most white major leaguers. Negro league teams became known for playing "shadowball." Shadowball was a sort of make-believe, imaginary baseball game, in which the teams would pretend to play baseball with an imaginary ball. They would exaggerate moves on the field as they threw the invisible ball. They would dive for the invisible "shadowball." They would run and leap like acrobats, to the delight of the crowds.

Negro league games often included contests such as home-run hitting and long-distance ball-throwing contests. No shadowballs here; players would challenge each other to throw the ball from home plate into the bleachers at the opposite end of the park. Even during the actual game, Negro league players would keep things fun and frisky by hitting a home run and then running the bases in reverse order starting from home plate and running to third, then second, first, and home.

The Negro Leagues

Negro league players often peppered their play with playful antics. Here, Horacio "the Rabbit" Martinez of the New York Cubans leaps to catch a ball between his legs.

Segregation and the Breakup of the Negro Leagues

The Negro league began to weaken in the 1940s. By 1945, African Americans and whites fought together in the newly desegregated American armed forces. Although segregation had always been unjust, it seemed even more unfair for African American men to risk their

Judy Johnson

lives defending a country that treated them as second-class citizens. After World War II, African Americans began to protest America's remaining segregation laws.

In 1945, the general manager of the Brooklyn Dodgers suggested the formation of the U.S. Baseball League, which allowed African American teams like the Brooklyn Brown Dodgers to play Ebbetts Field in New York while the Brooklyn Dodgers team was on the road. This was preparation for integrating African American ballplayers into the National League. The Negro National and American League teams regularly drew more fans to games, proving that African American players had the potential to be big attractions for fans.

In 1947, Jackie Robinson was signed by the Brooklyn Dodgers. This was a groundbreaking and symbolic act. As the first African American to be accepted into the major leagues, Robinson encountered plenty of racism. Even though America was changing, many people still didn't believe that African Americans should play

The Negro Leagues

major league baseball. In addition to being a great player, Robinson was also a charismatic, strong man who was capable of handling the pressure that came with being the only African American in a white league.

Other Negro league stars eventually followed Robinson into the major leagues. Although baseball integration was generally considered a positive move toward a unified country, it is important to realize how the African American community was affected. With their best players gone, Negro league teams suffered from a lower quality of play. Fans of all the old stars followed them in the major leagues. As a

Jackie Robinson

Judy Johnson

result, attendance at Negro league games dropped and finances were shaky. Negro league games had been such an important part of African American culture that when games stopped being popular, a sense of community was also lost.

By 1949, very few Negro league teams were making a profit. Their teams were being scouted for players like Satchel Paige and Jackie Robinson. They could no longer draw the huge crowds they used to draw ten or twenty years earlier. Owners of Negro league teams grew desperate and started selling off players to the major leagues in order to pay the bills. By 1950, major league teams were signing great African American players right and left. The Negro American League consisted of only four teams at that time: the Kansas City Monarchs, the Detroit Stars, the Birmingham Black Barons, and the Raleigh Tigers. In 1965, the U.S. Congress passed the Civil Rights Act, which forbade segregation in all public places. The following year, Red Sox great Ted Williams was inducted into the National Baseball Hall of Fame. In his acceptance speech, Williams made a point of criticizing the unfair lack of African American players in the Hall of Fame. The Negro league folded in 1968, shortly after the Indianapolis Clowns, the last original Negro league team, played its final game. It would be a long time before the major league Hall of Fame recognized and honored the great African American players of the 1930s and 1940s. For decades, these great players and their histories were essentially forgotten and ignored. Pitching great Satchel Paige wasn't even inducted into the Hall of Fame until 1971.

Comparing the Negro Leagues to the Major Leagues

Many people criticized Negro league baseball and claimed the white major leaguers played a better game. Some said the African American teams played baseball like minor leaguers and weren't as skilled as the white major leaguers were. Others said that Negro league players were far superior to their white counterparts. Since the two leagues were unequal in terms of salaries, playing fields, equipment, and general conditions, comparisons are unfair. However, it is interesting to note the differences.

Bench Strength

Some say the only difference between the African American leagues and the white major league was bench strength, or the number of players on a team. The white major league teams had about twenty-five players per team. The Negro league teams had about sixteen players per team. This meant that Negro league players didn't have the luxury of resting after a few innings.

Exciting Games

White baseball focused on either hitting balls out of the park or hitting base-to-base. The

The Negro Leagues

Like most Negro league teams, the Homestead Grays of 1949 consisted of sixteen players and a coach.

base-to-base playing method keeps the action to a minimum because the goal is to get runners from base to base, one play at a time. For example, a player at bat would aim for a base hit, or maybe he'd try to get walked to first base. He would then steal second base. The next batter up would bunt the pitch, allowing the player at second to advance to third base. The next player up would hit a single in order to score a run for the team. Overall, it was a generally effective strategy, but rather boring to watch. In contrast, Negro league baseball games were lively and entertaining. Players hit to almost any pitch thrown their way, and they also played with great flourishes and pageantry.

Physical Fitness and Stamina

Negro league players had remarkable stamina and often played well into their fifties. They were noted for being in better physical shape than were their white counterparts. White major leaguers generally took vacations after the season ended and were overweight and out of shape by spring training. Negro league players, however, were in top shape year-round from playing games constantly and taking little or no time off.

Another reason for African American players' superior physical fitness was that they got extra exercise by playing two positions on a team. Because they didn't have as many players on a team, African American baseball players had to do double duty, play more games, and take fewer

The Negro Leagues

breaks than did white major leaguers.

Salaries

Salaries of white baseball players averaged much higher than did Negro league players' salaries.

In the 1920s white players' salaries averaged $9,000 to $10,000 per year. African American players' salaries were much lower. They earned less than half of what white players earned, averaging about $1,200 to $3,000. But even though the Negro league players' salaries seem unfairly low, they earned far more money on average than African American men could earn in most other jobs in the 1920s through the 1950s.

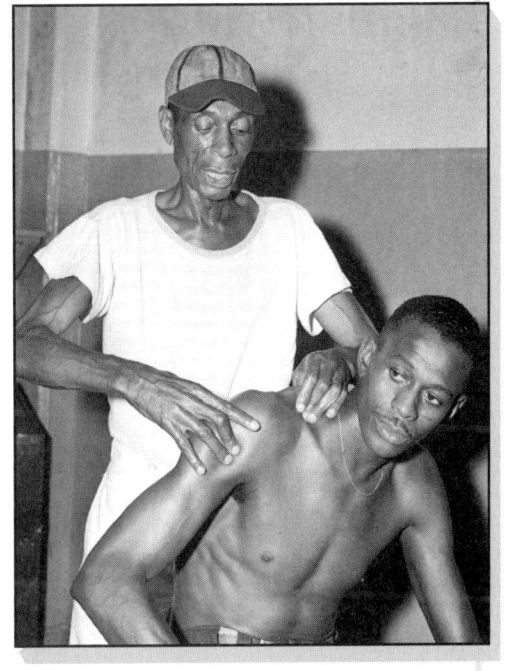

Satchel Paige gets a massage from Kansas City Monarchs trainer Frank Floyd, after performing in both games of a doubleheader.

Judy Johnson

Statistics

Negro league players were often left off lists of great baseball players simply because there weren't consistent statistics gathered for the Negro league games. Negro league teams could not afford to hire people to record the plays. Sometimes a player would start taking down the statistics, but then he might get pulled into the game and no one continued to record the statistics. The records would be incomplete. It's much easier to measure white baseball players' skills and achievements from that time because so many statistics were collected and saved for years.

However, when white major leaguers and Negro leaguers played each other during the off-season fall and winter games, statistics were kept. From 1900 to 1950, out of 436 interracial games, white teams won 168 games and African American teams won 268.

The Rookie

Judy Johnson quit Howard High School after tenth grade, primarily because he couldn't see the point in going through four years of high school if the school didn't have a baseball team he could join. Johnson left home, too, and got a job working as a stevedore, loading and unloading cargo on the docks in Deep Water Point, New Jersey. When the United States entered World War I in 1917 and sent troops to Europe, many African American baseball stars were drafted to fight in Europe. African American baseball teams lost a huge number of their best players to the war. At this time, Johnson was still a little too young to be drafted, so the timing was perfect for him to head to the top African American baseball teams. Johnson signed a contract with a New Jersey team, the Atlantic City Bacharach Giants, who paid him five dollars a day. Soon, Johnson became a sought-after player; while still playing for the Giants, he was asked to play on a second team, the Philadelphia Hilldales. Johnson played with the Hilldales in Darby, Pennsylvania, on Thursdays and Saturdays and with the Bacharach Giants in Atlantic City, New Jersey, on Sundays.

At the end of World War I, Johnson was sent to the Madison Stars, the minor league training ground for the Hilldales. The Hilldale Club had begun around 1912 as an amateur baseball club in the Philadelphia suburb of Darby, but by 1918 they were shaping up to be the top African American ball club in the East. The Madison Stars had only eleven players on the team. They played other teams in small towns in Pennsylvania and New Jersey.

It was at this time, while playing with the Madison Stars, that Johnson was given his nickname. One of the Madison Stars veterans, an outfielder named Robert Gans, went by the nickname Judy (no one seems to remember why). Everyone on the Madison Stars thought that Robert Gans and William Johnson looked just like each other, so the Madison Stars started calling William Johnson "Judy," too. The name stuck with Johnson for the rest of his life.

Playing in the Negro Leagues

Ed Bolden, a postal official who owned the Hilldales, asked Johnson to join the team officially and paid the Madison Stars $100 for him. Johnson was only twenty-one, the youngest player on the Hilldales. The youngest players with little to no playing experience are known as the team rookies. A player's rookie year is something like a teenager's first year in high school. He feels awkward and out of place and often is teased until he earns his teammates' respect. The older Hilldale players took many opportunities to remind Judy Johnson of his low

Judy Johnson

status as a team rookie. They often treated rookies as servants and ordered them to carry their equipment. Once, when the Hilldales were playing games in New York, the team decided to go to Harlem to enjoy the nightlife. On their way, the Hilldales' star slugger, Louis Santop, ordered Johnson to get off the subway train and make his way back to Grand Central Station in order to take a train back to Philadelphia with all of Santop's gear—his uniform roll and bats. There was too much stuff for one man to carry, so Johnson ended up having to take a taxi back to Grand Central Station. He didn't protest, partly because he knew he had to do what he was told, since rookies took orders from the stars on the team. Johnson knew he had to pay his dues.

Not everyone was so rough on Johnson. Veteran Hilldale player Bill "Brodie" Francis trained him to play third base, even though he must have known he was training the man who would replace him. Francis spent hours patiently teaching Johnson how to catch and field bunts. When he realized Johnson wasn't really getting the hang of

The Cotton Club, in the Harlem neighborhood of New York City, was a favorite nightspot of Negro league players visiting town.

it, he suggested that Johnson rush in and grab the ball with his bare hand and throw it all in one motion. That seemed to work for Johnson, who learned to throw underhand or across his body—whatever it took to make the play.

In 1921, the American Giants played the Hilldales. Johnson batted only .188, but the Hilldales signed him on to play every day. He was told that if he practiced hard all winter, he would be able to start as a regular on the team when the spring season began. When the spring season started in 1921, Johnson played his first game as an official Philadelphia Hilldale. Soon he was playing third base, replacing the man who had taught him how to field the ball, his kind and patient mentor Brodie Francis.

Winning Pennants with the Hilldales

The following year was a successful one for Johnson and for the Philadelphia Hilldales. After the departure of his mentor Brodie

The Rookie

Francis, Johnson looked to Hilldale veteran John Henry "Pop" Lloyd for guidance. Pop Lloyd nurtured Johnson's natural baseball gifts and taught him how to defend and protect himself. Lloyd taught Johnson how to play the ultimate defensive third-base position. His art of self-defense extended to protecting against the opposing team's sometimes violent trick of spiking basemen's legs with their shoe spikes in order to steal bases. Lloyd taught Johnson to wear shin guards to protect his legs from the sharp spikes of base runners' shoes. He also instructed Johnson in decoying base stealers. The trick was to pretend as though the ball wasn't coming to third base and then to tag out the runner at the last second. Johnson's 1922 average was .227.

In 1923, the Hilldales' team owner, Ed Bolden, formed the Eastern Colored League, taking some of the American Giants' best players and adding them to the Hilldale roster. Bolden added catcher Biz Mackey, hitter and first baseman George "Tank" Carr, and second

John Henry "Pop" Lloyd, player and manager of the 1923 Philadelphia Hilldales

The Rookie

baseman Frank Warfield to the Hilldales. Pop Lloyd played shortstop and managed the team. Bolden also bought Otto Briggs and Clint Thomas from Detroit teams. Bolden's signing binge of some of the best African American players around made the Hilldales' team roster an awesome lineup. At this point, the Hilldales were considered easily the strongest team in the East. Sure enough, they won the 1923 pennant, but they didn't go on to play the Negro League World Series.

Why didn't the Hilldales play in the 1923 Negro League World Series? Series promoter Rube Foster was so mad at Ed Bolden for taking his best players one by one over the course of 1923 to form the Eastern Colored League that he wouldn't let the Hilldales participate. Instead of playing the 1923 Negro League World Series, the Hilldales played exhibition games against various "temporary" teams made up of white major leaguers who didn't normally play together on the same team. Out of a total of nine exhibition games, the

Judy Johnson

Hilldales won seven games and lost only two against the white teams.

More Practice in the Off-Season

In the winter of 1923, Johnson went to Cuba to play baseball. He sharpened his batting skills there, facing some of the toughest pitchers he'd met up to that point in his career. As a result of this intense challenge and competition, he raised his batting average to .345.

When African American baseball teams played in Cuba, it was like playing in another world—a desegregated, nonracist world in which they were always treated as equals. In Cuba, African American baseball players received everything white major league ball players got—from hotels to restaurants to star treatment. If an African American baseball player was considered a great ball player, then he was given a hero's welcome. No African American baseball player was required to obey anything like a Jim

The Rookie

Crow law anywhere or anytime. Playing baseball in Cuba was like taking a vacation from racist America. It was a carefree time for many African American players, who got a rude awakening when they returned to the United States. Imagine meeting thunderous applause and praise from Cuban audiences while playing exhibition games in Cuba. Then imagine going back to America and its injustices.

It must have been hard to remember those ideal games in Cuba when Johnson and the Hilldales ran across what was easily Johnson's closest brush with a lynch mob. When the Hilldales played in a Pennsylvania coal mining town in the early 1920s, the game's umpire, who was also the very racist local sheriff, seemed to take sick pleasure in making the Hilldales as uncomfortable as possible. Hilldale catcher Louis Santop decided to get revenge on the racist umpire. Santop signaled for a high, hard fastball, then watched it burn through the air. He didn't even try to catch it! Of course, the fastball hit the umpire square on

Judy Johnson

the throat. The crowd went crazy. The entire Hilldales team was chased for five or six miles by an angry mob who wanted to punish them for Santop's trick.

In the summer of 1924, the Hilldales became Eastern Colored League champions for the second year in a row. Rube Foster agreed to have another Negro League World Series, which pitted the Hilldales against the Kansas City Monarchs. Rookie shortstop Jake Stephens was too nervous to be of much use, so Johnson was enlisted to play shortstop in his place. Biz Mackey played Johnson's usual position at third base. Although Mackey was a good player, he had little or no experience playing the position of third baseman. Mackey made a critical error: He failed to catch a hard ground ball. The mistake allowed two runners to score. In the end, the Monarchs won the World Series. But Johnson did his best and scored a total of sixteen hits, including a home run.

In 1925, Johnson hit .364 despite the fact that he suffered an injury that year. During

The Rookie

one game in which he played shortstop, he fractured an arm. The Hilldales won a third pennant and faced the Kansas City Monarchs again in the 1925 World Series. The first game of the series was hard on the Hilldales because it went twelve innings long. It must have been a tense time for Johnson, since he didn't get a hit the entire game. He managed to get two hits in the second game, but Kansas City went on to win that game. The third game was a turning point of the series. After nine innings, the two teams were tied at 1–1. But at the top of the tenth inning, Johnson came through with a single and ended up scoring three hits. The Hilldales won the third game and won the next two games, too. They went all the way and won the whole series, with Johnson averaging a fine .300.

Palm Beach

In the winter of 1925, Johnson went to play ball in Palm Beach, Florida. Many African

Judy Johnson

American baseball players went to Palm Beach to play ball in the off-season. It wasn't just winter training they went for, either. Actually, most players worked two jobs in bustling Palm Beach: They entertained hotel guests with baseball games and also waited tables at the hotel restaurants. Two of the biggest Palm Beach hotels, the Poinciana and the Breakers, hired African American baseball players to entertain guests with exhibition games and to wait on them at mealtimes. It seems odd that the players would do double duty playing ball and waiting tables, but the hotels paid very high wages. African American baseball players raked in a lot of money in pay and tips over the winter. Many also took on a third job, gambling or importing illegal rum from Cuba, but Judy Johnson played only on the baseball diamond. His clean image as a good guy focused on baseball and not on danger helped to secure his lifelong good reputation.

The Rookie

Hard Times for Judy

In 1926, Johnson averaged .302. The Hilldales lost the Eastern League pennant to the Bacharachs. Over the winter, Johnson went to Cuba and hit .372. The Hilldales played a four-game exhibition series against a team of white major leaguers and won three out of four games. They made more money per player than they would have earned playing the Negro League World Series. The best part for Johnson, however, wasn't the big cash award. He said that what he really loved was beating the white major leaguer Lefty Grove. Lefty Grove behaved like a hateful racist throughout the series. Johnson got his revenge by hitting the first pitch Lefty threw, driving the ball just over Lefty's head so that it knocked his cap off. To top it off, Johnson scored a single. He said that shut Lefty up for a while. For Johnson, getting the best of Lefty Grove was better than any financial reward. He went on to Cuba for the winter of

Josh Gibson of the Homestead Grays is tagged out at home plate during a Negro league game.

The Rookie

1926 and hit .327 there. But back in the States, Judy's average was only .228.

The downward slide continued for Johnson, and 1928 turned out to be a rough year, easily his toughest year ever with the Hilldales. Johnson's batting average slumped to .231. But things turned around in 1929, the year that would be his best ever. That year, Johnson averaged .401 and had the most hits of any batter in the Negro leagues.

The year 1929 also marked Johnson's final season with the Hilldales. The Homestead Grays signed him as both player and manager for $500 a month, his highest salary. One day, the Homestead Grays' catcher was injured and couldn't play the game scheduled that day. Always resourceful, Johnson recruited a fan from the stands to stand in for the injured catcher. This fan from the stands not only saved the day for the Grays, but turned out to be quite a catch himself! The eighteen-year-old fan was Josh Gibson, who would become one of the Grays' star players and who would be recognized decades later as one of

Josh Gibson is considered to be one of the best catchers in baseball history.

The Rookie

the best baseball players of all time when he was inducted into the National Baseball Hall of Fame. Johnson took Gibson under his wing. After every game, Gibson would ask Johnson, "How'd I look today?" and Johnson would give him a tutorial and a performance review. Johnson and Gibson's close relationship on the field extended to a warm, affectionate friendship off the field.

The 1930 Negro League World Series featured the Homestead Grays against the New York Lincoln Giants. The Grays won five games to the Giants' two. Johnson hit .286. The Negro National League folded that same year, after the death of founder Rube Foster. In 1931, Johnson left the Homestead Grays to join the Darby Daisies, a spin-off team of the Hilldales. But soon the Hilldales' salaries were cut entirely due to the Depression and owner Ed Bolden's financial difficulties. The Hilldale team players all had to split whatever ticket money was left after expenses were paid. In 1932, Johnson joined the Homestead Grays' crosstown rivals, the Pittsburgh Crawfords.

Highs and Lows

Judy Johnson's professional career really kicked into gear in 1932, when he left the Homestead Grays to join Gus Greenlee's Pittsburgh Crawfords. His move to the Crawfords put him in the spotlight. The Pittsburgh Crawfords were the team to watch in the early 1930s, and Gus Greenlee had a lot to do with the creation of this remarkable, winning team.

William "Gus" Greenlee, originally from Marion, North Carolina, made his name as a successful African American businessman in Pittsburgh, Pennsylvania, in the 1920s and 1930s. Greenlee made most of his fortune by running a big gambling business.

Judy Johnson *(right)* poses with other members of the
Pittsburgh Crawfords, Negro league champions of 1932.

Judy Johnson

The particular kind of gambling Greenlee specialized in managing was called numbers running. When a gambler played "the numbers," he would try to choose three digits from a wheel of numbers. The goal was to pick the number that the gambling establishment had chosen earlier as that day's winner. Management generally paid at odds of 500 to 1. Bets were cheap, so if a gambler bet a penny on the winning number, he would win about five dollars. Greenlee suffered no bad reputation for dabbling in numbers running. In fact, he was respected as an important businessman in the African American community. In 1925, Greenlee bought the Crawford Grille in Pittsburgh. The Crawford Grille's dance hall became a regular stop for African American jazz entertainers touring the country. The Grille featured famous performers such as trumpet player Louis Armstrong and the singing group the Mills Brothers. The Crawford Grille's success added to Greenlee's reputation as a much-admired businessman.

Highs and Lows

In 1930, Greenlee began investing money in one of Pittsburgh's best African American semiprofessional ball clubs, the Crawford Colored Giants. The team played at the Crawford Recreation Center near the Crawford Grille. Greenlee had high hopes for the Crawfords. He wanted to own the best African American baseball team in the country. He decided they needed to have the best if they were going to be the best. So in 1931, he set about building a baseball park. Greenlee Field had a seating capacity of 7,500 and was well equipped with locker-room facilities for both the home team and visitors. Before Greenlee Field was built, the Crawfords had to use the local YMCA as a locker room because the white managers of the local ballpark refused to let African American players use their facilities.

In 1931, Greenlee signed future Hall of Famer Leroy "Satchel" Paige to pitch for the Crawfords. By 1932, the Pittsburgh Crawfords included the impressive lineup of Sam Streeter, Jimmie Crutchfield, and Judy Johnson.

Judy Johnson

Greenlee got Judy Johnson for his team in 1932, when the financial pressures of the Depression began to hurt Johnson's team, the Homestead Grays. Greenlee also took Josh Gibson, the catcher whom Johnson had scouted from the stands a few years earlier, and Ted Page from the Homestead Grays. By 1932, Greenlee owned a powerhouse team.

In 1932, the Pittsburgh Crawfords won 100 games and lost only 37. Between March 25 and July 21, 1932, the Pittsburgh Crawfords played 94 games. They grew famous for their style on the field as well as for their stamina. And Gus Greenlee took care of them in high style. Not only did the Pittsburgh Crawfords have their own ballpark (something that was very rare for a Negro league team), but Greenlee provided the team with their own new bus to travel in. Greenlee set them up to barnstorm around the country, because he knew that he could make more money by having the team travel to games rather than have them spend most of their time playing home games in Pittsburgh. Sometimes

Highs and Lows

Judy Johnson *(second from left)* **poses with other members of the Pittsburgh Crawfords in front of the team bus in 1935.**

Greenlee even drove the bus himself. The Crawfords also had their own publicist, a sportswriter named John Clark, who regularly published reports in the newspaper the *Pittsburgh American,* updating fans on the Crawfords' latest news from the road. Few teams in the Negro leagues could boast of having it all—talented players such as Johnson, Gibson, Crutchfield, and Paige; loads of stamina and style; a ballpark and a bus of their own; and their very own publicist to publish their press releases in their local newspaper. It seemed as though the Crawfords were the best and had the best of everything that life in the Negro leagues could offer. The Crawfords' fan base even included entertainers performing at the Crawford Grille. Singing group the Mills Brothers became big fans of the Pittsburgh Crawfords and even posed for photographs dressed in Crawfords team uniforms.

Johnson described the Pittsburgh Crawfords as the best team he ever played on and praised their team spirit. He always appreciated how the Crawfords played well and got along well together. Miraculously, there was no jealousy among them, even though there were big stars on the team such as Satchel Paige and Cool Papa Bell. It was clear that everyone had the same goals in mind—to play baseball as a team and to win as a team. No one in the Crawfords was out to seek his own personal glory. If a Crawford scored or pitched a no-hitter or hit a

Highs and Lows

Pittsburgh Crawford players stand together on their home field during a warm-up.

grand slam, it was all for the team. There was no internal fighting for the spotlight; any amazing play was a play for the whole team.

In 1933, Gus Greenlee promoted the first Negro league all-star game, called the East-West Classic. The East-West Classic was scheduled to be played in Chicago in September of that year. Fans were asked to choose the all-star teams by voting. The largest

Playing Rough

The Negro leagues were known for their tricks—some dirty and others harmless. None of these stunts are allowed in baseball today!

- Sticking needles in the ball's laces.
- Grabbing a runner's belt to throw him off balance and make him stumble or fall.
- Hidden Ball Trick—A baseman hides the ball, moves the base, and touches the runner with the ball while he's off-base.
- Spiking—A runner tries to escape a baseman by jabbing his shins with sharp spikes or cleats.
- Throwing balls at a runner's head.

African American papers in Chicago and Pittsburgh held the election for team players. On September 10, 1933, rain and thunderstorms couldn't keep people away from the game. About 20,000 fans packed the stands at Chicago's Comiskey Park. The game was a magnet for African Americans, and Chicago became a popular vacation spot. The Chicago

Highs and Lows

East-West Classic was the place to be in '33 for baseball fans who were thrilled to stay at the city's Grand Hotel, the same hotel where the players stayed. The Union-Pacific Railway Company even added extra cars on its Chicago route to accommodate all the fans.

After the Classic, the Crawfords played road exhibitions for the rest of the year. In 1934, they played an exhibition series against a white team led by the major league World Series hero Dizzy Dean of the St. Louis Cardinals. The Crawfords beat the major league team three times and then won two more games in Dayton, Ohio. When the two teams met again at Yankee Stadium in New York, the umpire unfairly judged a play, telling the Crawfords, "You can do that in your league, not against white leaguers." Johnson averaged about .243 for the year in 1934.

In 1935, the Crawfords played the New York Cubans in the Negro League World Series. Johnson was in a slump for a while until he batted at the end of the ninth inning of the

Judy Johnson

game. The Crawfords were losing the seventh and final game of the series. At the bottom of the ninth inning, with two men on base and two out, Johnson came through with a clutch hit, sending a grounder past the first baseman. Josh Gibson and Oscar Charleston both hit home runs and ended the series in a glorious victory.

Members of the New York Cubans argue an umpire's call.

Highs and Lows

Johnson led the Crawfords to the Negro league title and was named team captain.

The following year was successful for Johnson and the Crawfords. They tied a team of major league all-stars in an exhibition game and won the season's second-half championship. Everything seemed to be going well for Johnson. That's why he was shocked when, in 1937, Greenlee traded him and Josh Gibson to the Homestead Grays in exchange for catcher Pepper Bassett, infielder Harry Spearman, and $2,500. Johnson was hurt and insulted and soon retired from professional baseball.

Life After the Crawfords

In 1937, Judy Johnson took a break from baseball. He took a job as a supervisor at the Continental Cab Company in Wilmington, Delaware. In his free time, he coached a team, but it wasn't a baseball team. Instead, it was a semiprofessional basketball team called the Alco Flashes. Under Johnson's direction they became the 1937 Delaware state champions. Around 1940, Johnson and his brother opened a general store together. He didn't spend much time at the store, however, because he went back to baseball as a scout for major league teams. Johnson went back to professional baseball around 1947, the year that Jackie Robinson broke the color barrier in

Judy Johnson *(second from left)* meets with other former Negro league stars at Ted Page's bowling alley in Pittsburgh, Pennsylvania, in 1953.

Judy Johnson

professional baseball and was signed to the Brooklyn Dodgers.

Johnson was a scout for several major league baseball teams. It's not surprising that he would become a scout: He had proven his eye for talent when he'd picked future Hall of Famer Josh Gibson out of the stands to fill in for the Grays' injured catcher. In 1951, Johnson was hired by the Philadelphia Athletics (the A's), and he scouted two young African American players, Bob Trice and Vic Power, into the major leagues. Johnson found the A's a player who could have been one of their greatest ever—future Hall of Famer Hank Aaron, who was then playing for the Indianapolis Clowns. Johnson woke his boss in the middle of the night and told him that he had a great recruit in mind and that $3,500 would be all it would take to sign him. But the owner refused, claiming that it was too much money. Of course, Johnson was right about Aaron, who went on to baseball fame and glory with the Atlanta Braves. Disappointed by the owner's foolish refusal to sign Aaron, Johnson

Life After the Crawfords

resigned his position with the A's in 1959 to scout for the Philadelphia Phillies.

Johnson went to Florida with the Phillies every year for spring training until 1974, when he finally retired. During spring training, Johnson helped to teach the ballplayers and improve their skills. Back in his day, he had been a good student, learning from older, more experienced ballplayers on his teams. When he first joined the Hilldales in 1920, Johnson paid attention to Brodie Francis, who taught him how to field balls. He also listened to Pop Lloyd, who taught him to play third base and to protect himself.

It was important to Johnson to be a good teacher for these young ballplayers. He once said that you have to take the time to show a player how to do something right. He said, "You can't just holler at him; you've got to show him how the ball is handled." Johnson compared baseball training to going to school. He said, "Baseball is like school; you get promoted if you learn." He also scouted for the Milwaukee

Judy Johnson

Braves, for whom he helped to sign outfielder Billy Bruton, who later became his son-in-law.

Many in baseball thought that Johnson's skills as a coach and instructor would have made him an outstanding baseball team manager. He had the rare ability to pinpoint exactly what a ballplayer was doing wrong and then help the player to correct it. Johnson loved to teach and coach. He said coaching was like putting a seed in the ground and watching it grow and develop. "As long as they're ballplayers," he said, "they're my kids. I love 'em all."

Induction into the Hall of Fame

In 1975, Judy Johnson was elected to baseball's Hall of Fame in Cooperstown, New York. This milestone in his career was an emotional time in his life. He was recognized for being one of the greatest baseball players of all time and of all races. No longer would his accomplishments be ignored or hidden

Life After the Crawfords

behind the shadow of a racially segregated baseball world or a racially segregated country. When the Hall of Fame inducted Johnson into its ranks, it gave him its highest honor. Johnson broke down in tears while giving his acceptance speech. His son-in-law, former Milwaukee Brave and Detroit Tiger Billy Bruton, rushed to Johnson's side as he cried into the microphone. Although overcome with emotion, Judy Johnson managed a brief and extremely moving speech as he uttered the plainspoken truth: "I am so grateful."

Judy Johnson said that, for most of his life, he never got too depressed about how rough life was for him and the other African American baseball players. He never developed a hateful resentment toward the men who upheld baseball's color barrier. He never regretted his suffering or envied the fame and high salaries of professional baseball players in the 1970s and 1980s. He had some sad moments though, moments so sad that they made him turn away from baseball.

Judy Johnson

After he was inducted into the Hall of Fame in 1975, Johnson stopped going to baseball games. He found himself becoming more and more disgusted by reports of baseball players' ever-rising salaries. It seemed to him that these new generations of baseball players cared more

Buck O'Neil, a former opponent of Johnson's, signs a baseball for fellow player Johnny Washington at a reunion of former Negro league players on November 17, 2000, at the Negro Leagues Baseball Museum in Kansas City, Missouri.

Life After the Crawfords

about their paychecks than about the game. In 1981, Johnson wrote a letter to *Sports Illustrated* to compliment a story about a reunion of some of his Negro league peers. The magazine published the letter in the July 6, 1981, issue, and also included his observations that the world of contemporary baseball was more of a grim business than the great game he had played in his youth. He wrote, "Negro league players of the earlier decades unfortunately were not recipients of enormous commercial residuals and bonuses. We played for something greater that could not be measured in dollars and cents. The secrets of our game were to enjoy and endure."

The National Baseball Hall of Fame

In the early 1900s, a baseball writer named Henry Chadwick wrote an article about the history of the game we know as baseball. Chadwick claimed that our baseball was a version of an old British ball game called rounders. Albert G. Spalding, one of baseball's early pioneers, read Chadwick's article and decided that the game's historical origins needed to be officially established once and for all. Spalding helped form a group of men to figure out where, when, and how the American sport of baseball began. In 1905, Spalding's group was made up of successful white businessmen and politicians, including Colonel A. G. Mills of New York (who played baseball during the Civil War era), the Honorable Morgan G. Bulkeley (former governor of Connecticut and the National League's first president in 1876), the Honorable Arthur Gorman (a senator from Maryland, a former player, and president of the National Baseball Club of Washington, D.C.), Nicholas E. Young (fifth president of the National League),

Alfred J. Reach of Philadelphia and George Wright of Boston (both businessmen and former baseball players), and James E. Sullivan of New York (president of the Amateur Athletic Union). This group was called the Mills Commission, and they researched baseball's historical roots for three years.

The Mills Commission finished its research in 1908, concluding that the founder of baseball was a Civil War veteran named Abner Doubleday. The commission received letters and documents that suggested that Doubleday had reinvented an old backyard game called town ball. Town ball was played in a field where as many as twenty to fifty boys competed to catch a ball hit by a "tosser" using a 4-inch flat bat. Records indicated that Doubleday turned "town ball" into the game we know as baseball by reducing the number of players, adding four bases for the batter to run around, and adding the positions of pitcher and catcher. The Mills Commission decided that Abner Doubleday created baseball in 1839 in Cooperstown, New York. The naming of Abner Doubleday as the father of baseball has been disputed by many.

Stephen C. Clark, the wealthy founder of the Singer Sewing Machine Company, bought an old baseball believed to date from 1839. He created a one-room exhibition in the Cooperstown Village Club for the old ball plus some other old baseball items. The tiny exhibition attracted so many visitors that Clark realized there was public demand for a national baseball museum to house baseball artifacts and honor its famous

Mrs. S. B. Hall *(left)*, Ford Frick, president of the National League, and Mrs. Ford Frick *(right)*, were among the notables attending the opener between the Giants and the Brooklyn Dodgers at Ebbets Field in Brooklyn, New York, on April 20, 1937.

players. Clark worked with baseball commissioners and league management to organize and establish the National Baseball Museum in Cooperstown. American baseball enthusiasts sent in money and baseball memorabilia from all over the country. By 1935, plans were underway to establish a national baseball museum in Cooperstown, New York, as the site of a celebration marking baseball's 100th anniversary. Ford Frick, the president of the National League, suggested that a hall of fame be established as part of the museum to honor baseball's greatest players. The Baseball Writers of America, an association of sports journalists, were asked to choose their picks for the best major league baseball players so that they could be honored at the 100th anniversary celebration. The Baseball Writers of America elected the following to the Hall of Fame: Ty Cobb, Babe Ruth, Honus Wagner, Christy Mathewson, and Walter Johnson. The National Baseball Hall of Fame and Museum was officially dedicated on June 12, 1939.

Remembering Judy Johnson

Judy Johnson died on June 15, 1989, in Wilmington, Delaware, at the age of ninety. It seems that anytime anyone had anything to say or write about him, they couldn't help but mention what a wonderful guy he was, not only as a baseball player, but also as a person. Everyone who knew him remembered him with great admiration and affection. The baseball history books are loaded with compliments and honors for Judy Johnson. Most of them praise his good character at the same time they praise his baseball skills. Clearly, Johnson distinguished himself for good sportsmanship. Cool Papa Bell described him as "a gentleman both on and off the field.

Judy Johnson is buried in Wilmington, Delaware, with his wife, Anita.

Judy Johnson

Nobody could push him around, but his quiet, easy, down-to-business manner made him a standout as a player and as a man." In an interview with Pittsburgh Crawfords biographer and historian James Bankes, Cool Papa Bell remembered Johnson well. He said, "Judy was the best. You could trust him in every way. I would trust him with my life and with my money. He would never let you down. He was always up and optimistic. He brought sunshine into your life. Judy and Jimmie Crutchfield are the two finest people I met in baseball."

Johnson was known for never losing his spirit. Even though he and his teammates often had plenty of reason to complain, or worry, or just quit, he never let anything really get him down. And, he tried hard to make sure nothing let his teammates down, either. He was always there to cheer them up, to encourage them, or lend a helping hand. Cool Papa Bell said that things often got very rough for the Pittsburgh Crawfords, and when they did, Bell remembered that Johnson always helped to make things

Cool Papa Bell poses with a bat after being inducted into the National Baseball Hall of Fame on February 14, 1974.

Judy Johnson

better. Bell said, "Judy would always say, 'Just keep goin' boys, the sun will be shining up there ahead someplace.'" Johnson was a tireless cheerleader for his teammates. He was always pointing out that even when things looked hopeless for them, as though they were under dark, cloudy skies, they should always remember that they would find the place where the sun was shining, where things would be better. This is no doubt why he was also known as Mr. Sunshine—because he was like a warm sun for his teammates, always spreading warmth, light, and hope.

Johnson always made an effort to do the right thing at all times. It didn't matter if it was something small or if it was a big deal; everyone could always count on him to be considerate, honest, kind, and fair. Not surprisingly, Johnson had incredibly good manners. When the Crawfords traveled to Houston, Texas, during a stop on one of their first barnstorming tours in the South, a rich Creole woman named Mother Mitchell served a

Nicknames

Judy Johnson and Judy Gans may have been the only players in the Negro league to be nicknamed "Judy," but they weren't the only ones to have nicknames. Check out some of the other nicknames of African American baseball pioneers:

Grover Cleveland "Buck" Alexander (Chicago Giants, Detroit Stars, Indianapolis ABCs, Cleveland Elites) 1923–1926

Theodore "Bubbles" Anderson (Kansas City Monarchs, Birmingham African American Barons, Washington Potomacs, Indianapolis ABCs) 1922–1925

Alfred "Buddy" Armour (St. Louis Stars, Indianapolis ABCs, New Orleans-St. Louis Stars, Cleveland Buckeyes, Chicago American Giants) 1936–1947

George W. "Georgia Rabbit" Ball (Cuban X-Giants) 1904–1905

Charles "Lefty" Bell (Homestead Grays) 1948

James "Cool Papa" Bell (St. Louis Stars, Pittsburgh Crawfords, Detroit Wolves, Kansas City Monarchs, Chicago American Giants, Memphis Red Sox, Homestead Grays) 1922–1946

Emmett "Scotty" Bowman (Philadelphia Giants, Leland Giants, Brooklyn Royal Giants) 1905–1912

"Black Bottom" Buford (Nashville Elite Giants, Cleveland Cubs, Detroit Stars, Louisville Red Caps) 1929–1934

Marlon "Sugar" Cain (Pittsburgh Crawfords, Brooklyn Royal Giants, Indianapolis Clowns) 1938–1949

Richard "Speed Ball" Cannon (St. Louis Stars, Nashville Elite Giants, Birmingham Black Barons, Louisville Red Caps) 1928–1934

George "Tank" Carr (Los Angeles White Sox, Kansas City Monarchs, Philadelphia Hilldales, Bacharach Giants) 1912–1934

John Henry "Pop" Lloyd (Macon Acmes, Cuban X-Giants, Philadelphia Giants, Leland Giants, Lincoln Giants, Chicago American Giants, Brooklyn Royal Giants, Columbus Buckeyes, Bacharach Giants, Philadelphia Hilldales, New York Black Yankees) 1905–1931

Raleigh "Biz" Mackey (Philadelphia Stars) 1933–1935

Buford "Geetchie" Meredith (Birmingham Black Barons, Nashville Elite Giants) 1924–1930

Leroy "Flash" Miller (Newark Dodgers, New York Black Yankees) 1935–1940

Leroy "Satchel" Paige (Chattanooga Black Lookouts, Birmingham Black Barons, Cleveland Cubs, Pittsburgh Crawfords, Kansas City Monarchs, New York Black

Yankees, Philadelphia Stars) 1926–1950

Norman "Turkey" Stearnes (Montgomery Grey Sox, Detroit Stars, Lincoln Giants, Cole's American Giants, Chicago American Giants, Philadelphia Stars, Kansas City Monarchs, Detroit Black Sox) 1921–1942

"Smokey" Joe Williams (San Antonio Bronchos, Leland Giants, Chicago Giants, Lincoln Giants, Chicago American Giants, Bacharach Giants, Brooklyn Royal Giants, Homestead Grays) 1897–1932

Smokey Joe Williams

Judson "Boojum" Wilson (Baltimore Black Sox, Homestead Grays, Philadelphia Stars) 1924–1945

Judy Johnson

big, multicourse dinner for the entire Crawfords team. Cool Papa Bell remembered the huge meal: "There was roast beef and fried chicken. Mashed potatoes and sweet potatoes. Home-baked bread. Several kinds of salad. For dessert, we had our choice of several kinds of pies and fruit of all kinds." Many restaurants wouldn't serve African American people, and the Negro league traveling teams often had to rely on kind people to help them. Johnson so appreciated the generosity of his hostess that he didn't forget it or take it for granted, even after the wonderful evening of fine dining was over. When the Crawfords returned to Pittsburgh, he wrote a thank-you letter to Mother Mitchell and sent it to her.

Negro league slugger and fellow Pittsburgh Crawfords teammate Ted Page admired Johnson's honesty and good character. Page remembered a time while the Crawfords were on a barnstorming tour in the early 1930s, and Johnson went to a barber to get a haircut. When he went to pay the barber afterward, he realized

Remembering Judy Johnson

that he was short one penny. He felt so bad that he insisted on walking all the way back to where the Crawfords were staying in town in order to find a penny in his luggage to pay the barber. Even though the barber insisted that he was perfectly happy to overlook the penny, Johnson walked a mile back to his lodgings, got a penny, and walked another mile back to the barber shop in order to pay the rest of his bill. Of course, back in the 1930s, a penny was worth much more than it is today, but it was still a very small amount of money. Ted Page said that the barber ended up going to the Pittsburgh Crawfords game that night and made a big deal out of what happened earlier that day in his shop. The barber pointed out Johnson on the field as the incredible guy who had walked a couple of extra miles out of his way just because he owed him one little cent. Page said that the barber pointed out Johnson to as many people as he could because Johnson made a huge and wonderful impression on him. The barber happily told everyone he could that that

Judy Johnson

man playing on the field, Judy Johnson, was the most honest man he'd ever seen in his life.

As much as Johnson was remembered for his sunny disposition and good character, he was also widely respected. He may have been nice, but he was no pushover. Johnson wasn't intimidated by runners trying to spike his legs as they ran to third. He didn't cave in to threats from other players. He could hold his own with great strength no matter how intense things got during a game.

Newt Allen, who played second base for the Kansas City Monarchs, remembered Johnson as a great ballplayer and a gentleman. Allen said that Johnson "was a gentleman all through those baseball years when baseball was just as rough as could be. He was the type of fellow that didn't try to hurt anyone." Allen noted that Johnson always commanded respect and that he never argued about anything or disputed strikes or plays on bases.

He wasn't only a great third baseman, he was also a clutch hitter, a player his teammates could rely on to get a hit at critical moments in the game. For example, if there was a man at third when Johnson came up to bat, he'd always get a hit to send the player at third running home to score a run for the team. Pittsburgh Crawford spitballer Sam Streeter remembered him as the best clutch hitter. Streeter said there were some great clutch hitters on the Crawfords, but although Oscar Charleston, Josh Gibson, and Jimmie Crutchfield were all good clutch hitters, they weren't as good as Judy Johnson. "Judy was the best of them all. When you had men on base, Judy was the guy you wanted up there," Streeter said. And, on top of that, Johnson was smart. Baseball historian James Bankes described him as a man of great baseball intelligence and a "brilliant defensive operative who commanded universal respect." Johnson was a smart ballplayer who was also a superb athlete. Slugger Ted Page said, "You talk about playing third base, Judy was better than anybody I ever saw. He had a powerful, accurate arm. He could do everything, come in for a ball, cut it off at the line, or range way over the shortstop hole. He was really something."

Johnson was also a great sign stealer. "Nobody stole more signs," Jimmie Crutchfield said. He could decode the hand signals given by the opposing team's manager. He managed to figure out these hand signals quickly, just by paying attention to the signaling for a few innings. Johnson could crack codes like a master spy and even come up with a few sly tricks of his own. Once he decoded the other team's secret signals, he would whistle his own coded message to his teammates. Johnson had the natural ability to anticipate plays. He could figure out ahead of time what the other team was going to do. Beneath his sunny disposition was a brilliantly intelligent ballplayer. Baseball historian Bankes noted that Johnson was a "steadying influence on the Pittsburgh Crawfords." He was serene, calm, and never upset by distractions or the stress of the game.

Being born into a certain time in American history worked against so many African

American baseball players. Judy Johnson may never have played for the major leagues, but he was fortunate enough to spend his life playing the game he loved. Regardless of low salaries, poor playing conditions, and rampant racism, he was able to rise above injustice and simply enjoy the game.

Timeline

- **October 26, 1899** William Julius Johnson is born in Snow Hill, Maryland, to parents William Henry and Annie Lee Johnson. Judy is the second of their three children.
- **1918** Plays on Bacharach Giants. Also placed on roster of the semipro Madison Stars. Acquires nickname Judy.
- **1919** Plays on Chester Stars.
- **1920** Trains on Madison Stars, a Hilldales farm team. Joins Hilldales.
- **1923** Hilldales win first Eastern Colored League pennant.
- **1924** Hilldales in Negro League World Series vs. Kansas City Monarchs.
- **1925** Philadelphia Hilldales play Negro League World Series vs. Kansas City.
- **1929** Johnson's final season with Philadelphia Hilldales (who become the Darby Daisies); serves as player-manager for the Homestead Grays.

Timeline

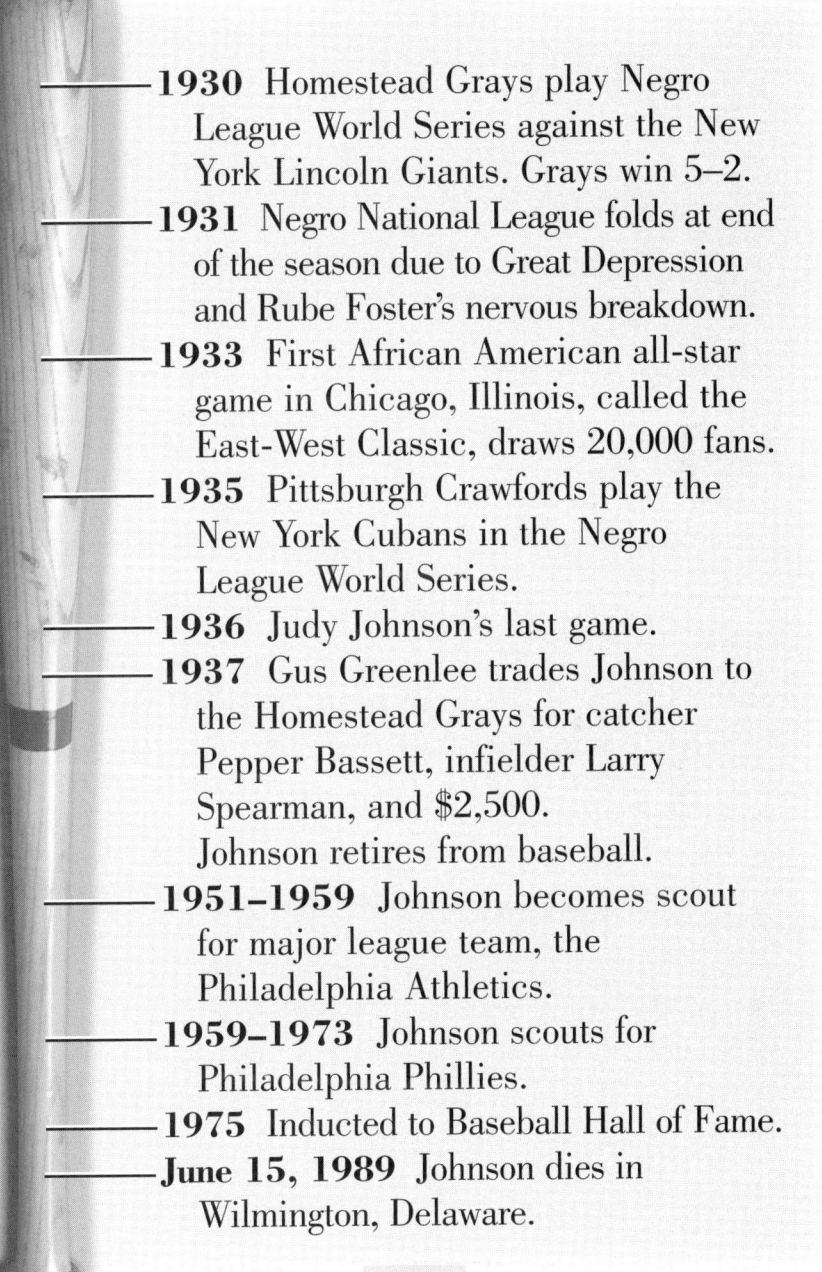

1930 Homestead Grays play Negro League World Series against the New York Lincoln Giants. Grays win 5–2.

1931 Negro National League folds at end of the season due to Great Depression and Rube Foster's nervous breakdown.

1933 First African American all-star game in Chicago, Illinois, called the East-West Classic, draws 20,000 fans.

1935 Pittsburgh Crawfords play the New York Cubans in the Negro League World Series.

1936 Judy Johnson's last game.

1937 Gus Greenlee trades Johnson to the Homestead Grays for catcher Pepper Bassett, infielder Larry Spearman, and $2,500. Johnson retires from baseball.

1951–1959 Johnson becomes scout for major league team, the Philadelphia Athletics.

1959–1973 Johnson scouts for Philadelphia Phillies.

1975 Inducted to Baseball Hall of Fame.

June 15, 1989 Johnson dies in Wilmington, Delaware.

Glossary

barnstorming Going on the road to play baseball games for many weeks or up to months at a time.

bunt Tapping a pitched ball lightly so it goes only into the infield.

clutch hitter Baseball player who always gets a hit to drive base runners home and score points.

commission Group of people given special authority or responsibility to complete a task or goal.

discrimination Treatment or judgement in favor of or against a group of people based not on what they earn or deserve but based only on what race, nationality, or gender they are.

Glossary

dry rot When a fungus infects material such as wood or leather, spreading throughout the material, leaving it dry, flaking, and falling apart.

exhibition Public display, show, or performance.

induct To place a person in a special, honored group or association in recognition of that person's achievements, skill, or talent.

integration Bringing together people of different racial or ethnic groups.

mentor Loyal, wise, and trusted counselor or teacher.

prejudice Irrational suspicion or hatred of a particular group, race, or religion.

rookie New player with little or no experience on a team.

settlement house Neighborhood house, often in a very poor neighborhood, where trained workers provide education, recreation, and community services.

scout Person, usually a former professional baseball player, who is hired by a professional, major league baseball team to travel to different cities and towns looking for new, young baseball players playing in minor leagues or in semiprofessional ballclubs.

screwball Baseball pitched with a reverse spin against the natural curve so it flies fast but not in a straight line.

segregation Keeping a group of people separated from the general body of society exclusively on the basis of race or nationality. Maintaining separate facilities for people of different races, nationalities, and sometimes even gender.

shadowball Name given to the imaginary baseball the Negro league players pretended to pitch, bat, and throw.

stamina Great physical strength.

statistics Numerical facts gathered and organized for future records.

stevedore Dock worker at a shipyard who loads and unloads cargo on and off ships.

veteran Person with a lot of experience on a team or at a job.

For More Information

National Baseball Hall of Fame, Museum, and
   Library and the A. Bartlett Giamatti
   Research Center
25 Main Street, P.O. Box 590
Cooperstown, NY 13326
(888) HALL-OF-FAME or (888) 425-5633
Web sites: http://baseballhalloffame.org
http://www.baseballhalloffame.org/
   library/research.htm

Negro Leagues Baseball Museum
1616 East 18th Street
Kansas City, MO 64108-1610
(816) 221-1920
Web site: http://www.nlbm.com

Web Sites

BaseballLibrary.com
http://cbs.sportsline.com/u/baseball/bol

Black Baseball's Negro Baseball Leagues
http://www.blackbaseball.com

Major League Baseball
http://www.mlb.com

Negro League Baseball
http://www.negroleaguebaseball.com

SABR (Society for American Baseball Research)
http://www.sabr.org

For Further Reading

Bankes, Jim. *The Pittsburgh Crawfords.* Jefferson, NC: McFarland and Co., 2001.

Gardner, Robert, and Dennis Shortelle. *The Forgotten Players: The Story of Black Baseball in America.* New York: Walker and Co., 1993.

Holway, John B. *Blackball Stars: Negro League Pioneers.* New York: Carroll and Graf, 1992.

Holway, John B. *The Complete Book of Baseball's Negro Leagues.* Fern Park, FL: Hastings House, 2001.

Peterson, Robert. *Only the Ball Was White.* New York: Gramercy Books, 1999.

Reidenbaugh, Lowell. *Cooperstown: Baseball's Hall of Fame.* New York: Gramercy Books, 1999.

Ward, Geoffrey C., and Ken Burns. *Shadowball: The History of the Negro Leagues.* New York: Alfred A. Knopf, 1994.

Index

A
Aaron, Hank, 76
Alco Flashes, 74
Allen, Newt, 96
American Giants, 48
Anson, Cap, 20, 22
Atlanta Black Crackers, 26
Atlanta Braves, 76
Atlantic City Bacharach
    Giants, 25, 44, 57

B
Baltimore African American
    Sox, 25
Bankes, James, 97–98
barnstorming, 30–31, 66
Bassett, Pepper, 73, 101
Bell, Cool Papa, 68, 86, 88,
    90, 94
bench strength, 38, 40
Birmingham Black Barons,
    26, 36

Bolden, Ed, 45, 49, 51, 61
Briggs, Otto, 51
Brooklyn Brown Dodgers, 34
Brooklyn Dodgers, 34, 76
Brooklyn Royal Giants, 25

C
Carr, George "Tank," 49
Charleston, Oscar, 72, 97
Chicago American Giants,
    23, 26
Civil Rights Act, 9, 36
Clark, John, 67
Columbus Blue Birds, 26
Crawford Colored Giants, 65
Crutchfield, Jimmie, 65, 67,
    88, 97–98
Cuban All Stars, 25

D
Darby Daisies, 61, 100
Dean, Dizzy, 71
Detroit Stars, 26, 36

E

Eastern Colored League (ECL), 25–26, 49, 51
East-West Classic, 69, 71, 101

F

Foster, Andrew "Rube," 23–26, 51, 54, 61,
Francis, Bill "Brodie," 46, 48, 77

G

Gans, Robert, 45
Gibson, Josh, 59, 66–67, 72–73, 76, 97
Greenlee, Gus, 26, 62, 64–67, 69, 73, 101
Greenlee Field, 65
Grove, Lefty, 57

H

Hilldale Club, 44
Homestead Grays, 26, 59, 61–62, 66, 73, 101
Hueston, Judge W. C., 26

I

Indianapolis ABCs, 26
Indianapolis Clowns, 31, 37, 76

J

Jacksonville Red Caps, 26

Johnson, Anita, 19
Johnson, Annie Lee, 10, 100
Johnson, Mary Emma, 12–13
Johnson, William Henry, 10–13, 15, 100
Johnson, William Julius "Judy,"
  baseball scout, 74, 76–78
  batting slump, 59, 71
  birth, 10, 100
  coaching, 77–78
  death, 86, 101
  Hall of Fame, 78–79, 101
  Howard High School, 43
  retired from baseball, 73–74
  traded to Homestead Grays, 73, 101
  work as a stevedore, 43

K

Kansas City Monarchs, 25, 36, 54–55, 96

L

Lincoln Giants, 25, 61, 101
Lloyd, John Henry "Pop," 49, 51, 77

M

Mackey, Biz, 49, 92
Madison Stars, 44–45
Memphis Red Sox, 26
Mitchell, Mother, 90, 94

Index

N
National Baseball Hall of Fame, 37, 61, 85
Negro American League, 26, 34, 36
Negro League World Series, 51, 54, 57, 61, 71, 100–101
Negro National League, 25–26, 34, 101
Negro Southern League, 26
New York Cubans, 71

P
Page, Ted, 66, 94, 97
Paige, Satchel, 36–37, 65, 67–68
Philadelphia Athletics (A's), 76
Philadelphia Hilldales, 25, 44–45, 48, 51–55, 59, 100
Philadelphia Phillies, 77
Pittsburgh Crawfords, 26, 61–62, 66, 68–73, 88, 90, 94–95
Power, Vic, 76

R
Raleigh Tigers, 36
Robinson, Jackie, 34–36, 74
Rosedales, 18
Royal Blues, 15

S
salaries, 41, 80–81
Santop, Louis, 46, 53
segregation, 6–8, 33–34
 in baseball, 22–23, 52–53
 Jim Crow laws, 8–9, 29
 Plessy v. Ferguson, 6–7, 22
shadowball, 32
Spearman, Harry, 73, 101
statistics, 42
Streeter, Sam, 65, 97

T
Texas Negro League, 26
Thomas, Clint, 51
Toledo Blue Stockings, 20
Trice, Bob, 76

W
Walker, Moses Fleetwood, 20
Warfield, Frank, 51
Williams, Ted, 37
winter leagues, 28–30, 52

Z
Zulu Giants, 31

About the Author

Kathleen Billus earned her undergraduate degree in English at Smith College in Northampton, Massachusetts. She has worked in publishing, as a writer and an editor for print and online magazines (*Sick-n-Tired, Escargot: Music,* and the *Internet*), managed bands, run fan clubs, taught, and traveled internationally. She currently works for a nonprofit company that produces and distributes educational video and telecourses for distance learning. Writing a book about Judy Johnson combined her lifelong passion for reading and writing and her love of baseball. Billus is happy to be a short drive away from Dodger Stadium and to have a good friend with season tickets.

Photo Credits

Cover, p. 4 © New York Public Library; pp. 7, 8, 47, 75 © Hulton Archives; pp. 17, 21, 27, 29, 33, 35, 41, 58, 69, 72, 84 © Corbis; p. 39 © Carnegie Library of Pittsburgh; pp. 50, 60, 63, 67, 80, 89, 93 © AP/Wide World Photos; p. 87 © Jane Smith.

Design

Claudia Carlson

Layout

Nelson Sá